HISTORY THROUGH SOURCES
The Western Front

RIGBY INTERACTIVE LIBRARY

Rosemary Rees

RIGBY INTERACTIVE LIBRARY

Published by Rigby Interactive Library an imprint
of Reed Educational & Professional Publishing,
500 Coventry Lane, Crystal Lake, IL 60014

Produced by Mandarin Offset Ltd., Hong Kong
Printed in China
02 01 00 99 98

10 9 8 7 6 5 4 3 2 1

**Library of Congress Cataloging-in-Publication
Data**
Rees, Rosemary, 1942-
    The Western Front / Rosemary Rees:
    [illustrated by Jeff Edwards].
        p. cm. -- (Heinemann history depth studies)
    Includes bibliographical references and index.
    Summary: Discusses reasons for Allied victories
    on the Western Front during 1914–1918;
    describes trench warfare, coping strategies, and
    the role of women; shows how these campaigns
    are remembered.
    ISBN 1-57572-217-8 (lib. bind.).
    1. World War, 1914–1918--Campaigns--Western
Front--Juvenile literature.   2. World War,
1914–1918--United States--Juvenile literature.
[1. World War, 1914–1918--Campaigns--Western
Front.   2. World War, 1914–1918--United
States.]   I. Edwards, Jeff, ill.   II. Title.
III. Series.
D530.R38   1997
940.4'272--dc21   97-4476
                                                 CIP
                                                  AC

Designed by Ron Kamen, Green Door Design

Illustrated by Jeff Edwards

Front cover: American Troops in a Renault Tank
(Corbis-Bettman)

Acknowledgments

The author and publisher would like to thank the
following for permission to reproduce poems and
songs:

Michael Hamburger and Carcanet/Persea Books:
'Battlefield' (page 43)
Macmillan London Ltd: 'Breakfast' by Wilfred Gibson
(page 24)
George Sassoon: 'Aftermath' (page 43)
Canoflan Sain: 'Tommy's gone away' (page 29)

Every effort has been made to contact copyright
holders of any material reproduced in this book. Any
omissions will be rectified in subsequent printings if
notice is given to the publisher.

Details of written sources

In some sources the wording or sentence structure
has been simplified to ensure that the source is
accessible.

C. Barnett, *The Swordbearers*, Eyre & Spottiswoode,
1963: 1.16
Vera Brittain, *Testament of Youth*, Victor Gollancz,
1933: 5.2
Malcolm Brown, *The First World War*, Guild, 1991:
1.3, 3.17, 3.18, 3.19, 5.2, 5.6
J. Ellis, *Eye Deep in Hell*, Croom Helm, 1976 4.4
Wilfred Gibson, *Collected Poems 1905–1925*,
Macmillan & Co, 1926: 3.3
Nigel Kelly, *The First World War*, Heinemann, 1989:
1.8, 2.3, 2.4
Lyn Macdonald, *Voices and Images of the Great War*,
Allen Lane / Penguin, 1991: 2.10, 3.10, 3.14, 4.6
M. Middlebrook, *First Day on the Somme*, Allen Lane,
1971: 1.12
R. A. Rees, *Britain and the Great War*, Heinemann,
1993: 1.18
Norman Stone, *The Eastern Front 1914–17*, Hodder
and Stoughton, 1975: 2.12
A. J. P. Taylor, *The First World War*, Penguin, 1963:
1.7, 1.13
John Terraine, *Douglas Haig, the educated soldier*,
Hutchinson, 1962: 1.1, 1.11
Denis Winter, *Death's Men: Soldiers of the Great War*,
Allen Lane, 1978: 2.6, 3.2, 3.8, 3.15, 4.7, 4.11
J. M. Winter, *The Experience of World War I*,
Macmillan, 1988: 1.20, 2.2, 2.8, 3.12

Note

In this book some of the words are printed in **bold**
type. This indicates that the word is listed in the
glossary on page 47.

The glossary gives a brief explanation of words that
may be new to you.

The author and publisher would like to thank the
following for permission to reproduce photographs:

Bridgeman Art Library: 6.4
Camera Press: 1.10
Illustrated London News Picture Library: 3.4
Imperial War Museum: 1.2, 1.4, 1.14, 1.19, 1.21, 2.1,
2.5, 2.7, 3.1, 3.11, 3.16, 4.2, 4.8, 5.1, 5.3, 5.4, 6.3
Jean Loup Charmet: 1.9
Kobal Collection: 6.1
Peter Newark's Military Pictures: 1.6
Ullstein Bilderdienst: 1.5

Contents

Why Did the Allies Win on the Western Front?

Was the the Western Front important?

When you think about World War I what picture comes into your mind? The sinking of the *Lusitania*? T. E. Lawrence, galloping across the deserts of Arabia? Or the mud of northern France, with soldiers struggling to "go over the top" of their trenches to attack the enemy? Most people remember the mud, the death, and the trenches of the Western Front. Why? The British and French generals believed that the Western Front was critical in the war, because only there could Germany be defeated. In addition, on the Western Front the most terrible slaughter of young men took place, as they fought to take and retake a few hundred yards of mud.

These young men wrote diaries, letters, and poems that still haunt us. They show us the helplessness of generals and soldiers who were trapped in a situation they didn't understand and from which they couldn't escape.

HOLLAND

N

London

Messines

Ypres

Ypres

Messines

BELGIUM

GERMANY

Neuve-Chapelle

Loos

Vimy Ridge

Arras

Somme R.

Cambrai

Cambrai

Somme

LUXEMBOURG

Aisne R.

Champagne

Marne R.

Verdun

Paris

Verdun

FRANCE

Seine R.

→ Allied attacks
← German attacks
— Trenches
▨ Territory occupied by Germany 1914–18

0   100 km

The main battlefields of the Western Front, 1914–17

How was the Schlieffen Plan defeated?

The Schlieffen Plan depended on speed for its success. It aimed to knock France out of the war before Russia could fully **mobilize**. The Plan had been devised by Alfred von Schlieffen (Chief of the German general staff, 1891–1906) and put into action by his successor, General Helmuth von Moltke. Three-quarters of the entire German army was to make a gigantic westward sweep through Belgium and Luxemburg, and then swing southward around Paris. The whole operation was to take exactly 42 days.

SOURCE 1

We cannot hope to win until we have defeated the German army. The easiest place to do this is in France, because our lines of communication are the shortest to this theater of war.

Diary of Field-Marshall Sir Douglas Haig, when he was commanding the First Corps of the BEF, March 28, 1915

At first everything went as planned. By August 3 Luxemburg was occupied by German troops. On August 4 German army units swept into Belgium. Part of the German army was held up at Liege, which only surrendered after an eleven-day siege. Meanwhile, on August 20, other German troops under General von Kluck entered Brussels.

The German troops then headed south. The **British Expeditionary Force** (BEF) managed to slow them down at Mons and Le Cateau, but by August 29, von Kluck's units were on the move again. They were forced to begin their swing south while still north of Paris. They did this in order to keep in touch with the German units that had been held up at Liege, and because they thought the BEF had blocked their planned route.

Meanwhile, Russia had mobilized more quickly than the German commanders had expected, and von Moltke was forced to divert German troops to the Eastern Front. A new **Allied** line of French and British troops was formed just south of the Marne River. There, between September 5 and 10, they stopped the German advance at the First Battle of the Marne. The Germans retreated to the Aisne River. They dug themselves into deep defensive trenches so that enemy fire could not reach them. The Schlieffen Plan had failed.

Stalemate

Look carefully at the map on page 4. The German army was well into France. The British and French armies were backed up along the Marne River. If the German army could get round the Allied troops, it could surround them and trap them. If the Allied armies could get round the German troops, then they would be surrounded and trapped. Both sides tried to do this. They raced through northern France towards the Channel, fighting a series of battles as they tried to **outflank** each other. Historians call this "The

Germans digging their first trenches in late 1914

THINK IT THROUGH

The Schlieffen Plan failed for many reasons. Which was the most important?

Race to the Sea." The most bloody fighting was around Ypres, which was eventually held by British and French forces. By November 1914, of the original 160,000 members of the BEF, 90,000 had become casualties and 250,000 French and 130,000 German soldiers had either been killed or wounded. Neither side managed to outflank the other. Both sides dug trenches to defend themselves and stop the other side from advancing. A line of trenches stretched from the Belgian coast to the Swiss frontier. It was **stalemate**. The effort to break this stalemate is the story of the Western Front.

Why was Sir John French fired as commander of the British Expeditionary Force?

Sir John French commanded the 160,000 men of the British Expeditionary Force. He was sixty-six years old and a distinguished cavalry officer. Just over sixteen months later, in December 1915, he was asked to resign. What went wrong, and whose fault was it?

Sir John French's instructions were to support and cooperate with the French army. He planned a series of **diversionary attacks**. On March 10, 1915, the BEF attacked German army units at Neuve Chapelle. The British were short of shells, and could not afford to carry out the barrage that usually came before an attack. Instead, they went straight on the **offensive**. This took the Germans by surprise, and the British infantry broke through the German line. Once through, the British troops didn't know what to do next. They decided to wait for reinforcements, which never came. Meanwhile, German reinforcements arrived and filled in the gap. Sir John French ordered the British troops to continue battering away at the German line. The battle lasted three days. Nothing was gained by either side. Sir John French blamed the failure on the lack of shells. In turn, the British government blamed the **munition** workers.

The Battle of Neuve Chapelle was important because it set the pattern for what was to come: success at the beginning of a battle, which then led nowhere, followed by attack after attack even when the attacks gained no ground.

SOURCE 3

After a while there passed through the gate a handful of men in tattered uniforms, their faces blackened and unshaven, their clothes stained red with blood or yellow with the fumes of lyddite [a type of explosive]. I shouted for Y company—one man came forward. It was heartbreaking.

Gradually others tottered in, some wounded, all in the last stages of exhaustion, and when at last I went to lie down at about 5:30 A.M., there were in camp only 25 of my 130 men who had gone out six hours before. Since then the number has risen to a little over 40, and I know of 11 killed and 68 wounded but 25 are "missing." Some will doubtless turn up in hospitals; others may now be prisoners in Germany, but most, I fear, will be among the unidentified dead. Two officers survive, one belonging to my company who had to go to the Headquarters sick at an early stage of the battle. All my sergeants are gone, eight of them, and at the present moment I have for NCOs only two corporals and one lance-corporal. It is terrible: the regiment is practically wiped out.

Color-Quartermaster-Sergeant Robert Scott Macfie describes what happened after action at Hooge, near Ypres, on June 16, 1915.

SOURCE 4

A rare photograph of a battle in progress shows part of Robert Macfie's regiment, the Liverpool Scottish, during the action at Hooge on June 16, 1915.

Sir John French planned other diversionary attacks throughout the summer of 1915. Their aim was to draw the German army away from attacking French troops. British offensives at Aubers Ridge and Festubert, however, gained nothing. Sources 3 and 4 tell you what happened at Hooge. The Germans attacked only once at Ypres in April. They forced a gap in the British line, but then their advance stopped. Still Sir John French persisted, insisting on counterattacks. The only effect these had was to lengthen the casualty lists.

A photograph of the town of Loos, taken from the air after the battle, in 1917

By autumn, men and materials were exhausted and a "quick victory" for the Allies seemed impossible. General Joffre, the French Commander-in-Chief, wanted an allied autumn offensive in northern France. He asked the British to attack the German front line at the town of Loos. Sir John French objected, saying that that this would mean attacking across coalfields and through miners' cottages—a very difficult battlefield. However, Lord Kitchener, the British Secretary for War, insisted that Sir John French follow Joffre's directive. General Haig, who commanded the First Corps of the BEF, agreed. He was convinced the British would be victorious at Loos.

There were 15,000 British casualties on the first day of action. Despite this, British troops broke through the German front line and almost through the second line. Haig called for reserves. However, Sir John French kept the reserve troops far away in the rear. It took time to get them to the battlefield. In doing so they mixed with troops leaving the front line. In the confusion, German troops counterattacked and the British line was threatened with a breakthrough. The offensive ended in early November. The slaughter was terrible. Nothing had been gained. Sir John French blamed Haig for the confusion over the reserves at Loos, and therefore for the loss of the battle itself.

Meanwhile, Haig had not been loyal to Sir John French. He complained about French's failures to the Prime Minister, Herbert Asquith, and to anyone else of importance who would listen. He wrote about them to King George V. Finally, in December 1915, the government recalled Sir John French. He was replaced by Field-Marshal Sir Douglas Haig.

THINK IT THROUGH

In 1914 Haig wrote: "In my own heart I know that French is quite unfit for this great command at a time of crisis in our Nation's history."

Did events prove him right?

Three great battles: but who won?

By 1916 the British Commander-in-Chief, Douglas Haig, was convinced that an Allied offensive in northern France could succeed. The British army was growing into a huge force. Thousands of young men were volunteering to fight alongside the regular army. There were 139 Allied divisions in France (of which 38 were British) against only 117 German divisions. The French Commander-in-Chief, Joffre, suggested a combined summer offensive by the Somme River, where the British and French front lines joined. By then, the Allies would have far more soldiers in the field than the Germans and would be bound to win. The German Commander-in-Chief, Falkenhayn, however, had other plans. He decided that the way to win the war was by a policy of attrition. The enemy would be worn down so that their men and materials were exhausted before those of the Germans. Falkenhayn wanted to weaken the French army so much that France could not continue fighting and would drop out of the war. Without a continental ally, Britian would then be forced to make peace with Germany.

Verdun

Falkenhayn needed to find a target so important to the French that they would fight to the end to defend it. He chose the fortress of Verdun. This fortress held a special place in French history and in the hearts of French people. It symbolized their resistance to invasion. The French generals, however, did not think Verdun was particularly important. They had had most of Verdun's guns removed for use elsewhere on the Western Front. Indeed, they argued with the politicians that it wouldn't really matter if Verdun fell, and that it certainly wasn't worth wasting the lives of French soldiers to defend it. The politicians thought differently.

On February 21, 1916, the German army fired more than a million shells at French positions in the forts around Verdun. On February 25, Fort Douaumont fell to the German army. The next day, General Henri-Philippe Pétain, Commander of the French Second Army, was put in charge of the defense of Verdun.

YOUR KING & COUNTRY NEED YOU

A WEE "SCRAP O' PAPER" IS BRITAIN'S BOND.

TO MAINTAIN THE HONOUR AND GLORY OF THE BRITISH EMPIRE

A World War I British recruiting poster, 1916

If you surrender Verdun, you will be cowards, cowards! And you needn't wait till then to hand in your resignation. If you abandon Verdun, I sack you all on the spot.

Aristide Briand, Prime Minister of France, talking to Joffre and his staff

They won't get through.

Said by General Pétain, when put in charge of the defense of Verdun

The French defended Verdun with all their might. Between February 21 and the end of June 1916, when the fighting died away, 78 divisions of the French army were diverted to Verdun. This was exactly what Falkenhayn had hoped for. However, the more the French resisted, the more important it became to the Germans that they took Verdun. The battle turned into a slaughter.

Throughout the spring, assaults and bombardments got stronger; both **flamethrowers** and phosgene gas were used. On June 7, Fort Vaux fell to the Germans. By the end of June, when the fighting began to die away, 542,000 Frenchmen and 434,000 Germans had been killed, wounded, or reported missing. Fighting went on, but far less fiercely, until November 1916. Falkenhayn almost achieved his aims. The French fighting spirit was shattered by Verdun, and many units were close to mutiny. On the other hand, Verdun had not fallen, and many French soldiers looked on this as a victory. Pétain's reputation was made. He later became a marshal of France and head of the French state.

The key to the defense of Verdun was supplies. There was only one road in, and down this road trucks ferried supplies at the rate of 3,000 trucks per day. The French called this lifeline the "Voie Sacrée" (Sacred Route).

The Somme

On July 1, 1916 the Allies launched their planned attack near the Somme River. Of all the generals involved on the Allied side, only Haig really believed that this was the attack that would win the war. The Germans held the high ground surrounding the river. Any attackers would have to fight their way uphill against a hidden enemy. By the summer of 1916 the German front line was heavily fortified. Their second line was just as strong, with dugouts 13 yards deep in the chalky ground. Even an experienced army of professional soldiers would have had difficulty in forcing such a line. The Allied troops were far from experienced. The 25 divisions of British soldiers were mainly made up of enthusiastic volunteers. They had had very little training; they couldn't shoot straight, and they had been taught that the only way to advance was slowly and in a straight line. The junior officers were also recruits, who had been taught to obey unquestioningly and never to show initiative. This great volunteer army was therefore neither flexible enough nor skilled enough to respond quickly to changes in the heat of battle. The original idea had been for French and British troops to fight side by side. However, Verdun had drained the French army so much that only five divisions could be spared to fight on the Somme. Thus, the success or failure of the battle fell mainly on the shoulders of the British.

The Battle of the Somme began with a seven-day bombardment. At the end of this, Haig was confident that the German front line trench system had been smashed. In fact, the bombardment failed. The German wire had not been destroyed. The German soldiers had simply retreated to their deep, second-line trenches, where they waited.

Wave after wave of British troops left their trenches on July 1, confident that victory would soon be theirs. In fact, they were mown down by machine-gun fire as they advanced slowly, with 66 pounds of equipment on their backs, toward the German trenches. By the end of the first day, 57,470 Allied and 8,000 German soldiers were dead or wounded. They were the worst casualties suffered by the British army on any day, ever. Haig saw no reason to change his tactics. By November, both sides were exhausted; 620,000 Allied and 450,000 German soldiers had been killed or wounded. At most, the Allies had advanced 5 miles along the Western Front.

SOURCE 11

The men are in splendid spirits. Several have said that they have never been so instructed and informed of the nature of the operations before them. The wire has never been so well cut, nor the artillery preparation so thorough.

Extract from the diary of Field-Marshall Douglas Haig, Commander of the BEF, written on June 30, 1916

SOURCE 12

It was pure bloody murder. Douglas Haig should have been hung, drawn, and quartered for what he did on the Somme. The cream of British manhood was shattered in less than six hours.

Private P. Smith of the First Border Regiment, July 1916

SOURCE 13

Idealism perished on the Somme. The enthusiastic volunteers were enthusiastic no longer. They had lost faith in their cause, in their leaders, in everything except loyalty to their fighting comrades. The war ceased to have a purpose. It went on for its own sake, as a contest in endurance. The Somme set the picture by which future generations saw the First World War: brave, helpless soldiers; blundering, obstinate generals; nothing achieved. After the Somme men decided that the war would go on forever.

A.J.P. Taylor, The First World War, 1963

SOURCE 10

After the Battle of the Somme, November 1916

Passchendaele

In December 1916, David Lloyd George replaced Herbert Asquith as Prime Minister of Great Britain. It seemed as though no more expensive attacks would be allowed. Lloyd George made it quite clear that he was not willing to send thousands more young men to their deaths with no certainty of gaining anything significant. He said he was not prepared to be a butcher's boy sending cattle to market. However, Haig had drawn up plans for a British offensive north of Ypres. The **Cabinet** was doubtful. Between April 29 and June 10, 1917, there had been 55 mutinies in the French army. France appeared to be an uncertain ally. In the end, the Cabinet decided that Haig's offensive just might pull the French army together and clear the Belgian coast of German troops.

The Third Battle of Ypres, often called Passchendaele, began on July 31, 1917. The Ypres **salient** was a disastrous place from which to launch an attack: it was surrounded on three sides by the German army. Again, commanders depended too much on the artillery bombardment and barrage, and didn't pay nearly enough attention to the land over which their soldiers were fighting. There were some successes: at the Menin Road and Polygon Wood, British objectives were achieved. By October, bad weather had set in and constant shelling had destroyed the land drainage systems. The battlefield became a sea of mud. When the Canadians finally took the village of Passchendaele, on November 6, it had been wiped out. On November 10, a halt was called. The British army had suffered 250,000 casualties. Most of these were volunteers in Kitchener's Army and Pals Battalions. None of Haig's objectives had been achieved.

SOURCE *14*

Canadian troops on the way to victory at Passchendaele, November 1917

FRENCH

Sir John French (1852–1925) joined the navy in 1866, but transferred to the army eight years later. He fought in the Sudan (1884–5) and as a cavalry officer in South Africa. He was Chief of the General Staff (1911–14) and was chosen to command the British Expeditionary Force in France in 1914.

At the end of 1915 he was moved back to Britain because of the disasters at Ypres, especially the battle of Loos where more British than Germans were killed and nothing was gained. Like most cavalry officers, he had no idea how to fight this new kind of war.

What difference did American troops make?

In November 1917 the Battle of Passchendaele ended. At the time it seemed impossible that a year and a day later Germany would surrender and the war would be over. How did this happen? Was it, as some historians have argued, all due to the entry of the United States into the war?

In a sense, the United States had been at war with Germany for a long time. The United States had supplied Britain with money, food, and raw materials for industry since the start of the fighting. American merchant ships had carried these goods across the Atlantic escorted by American naval ships. The German High Command had to stop these supplies from reaching Britain. In February 1917 Germany began unrestricted submarine warfare. This meant that German submarines attacked any ships anywhere which they suspected of carrying goods to Britain. American ships would be sunk, and the German High Command knew that they were running a tremendous risk. The risk was that the United States would declare war on Germany. If Britain and France were supported by the tremendous resources of the United States, German defeat would be very likely. However, the German High Command hoped that the whole situation would change before the United States declared war. They hoped Britain would be starved into submission. A starving Britain would be forced to ask for peace. It was a desperate gamble and it failed. On April 6, 1917, the United States declared war on Germany. Britain and France were still fighting. No one had asked for peace.

SOURCE 16

Our general situation requires that we should strike at the earliest moment, if possible before the end of February or the beginning of March, before the Americans can throw strong forces into the scale. We must beat the British.

General Ludendorff, speaking at a German war conference held at Mons on November 11, 1917

SOURCE 15

Three weeks ago today the enemy began his terrific attacks against us on a fifty-mile front. His objects are to separate us from the French, to take the Channel Ports, and destroy the British Army.

In spite of throwing already 106 divisions into the battle and enduring the most reckless sacrifice of human life, he has yet made little progress towards his goals.

We owe this to the determined fighting and self-sacrifice of our troops. Words fail me to express the admiration which I feel for the splendid resistance offered by all ranks of our Army under the most trying circumstances.

Many amongst us are now tired. To those I would say that victory will belong to the side which holds out the longest. The French army is moving rapidly and in great force to our support.

There is no other course to us but to fight it out. Every position must be held to the last man: there must be no retirement. With our backs to the wall and believing in the justice of our cause, each one of us must fight on to the end. The safety of our homes and the freedom of mankind alike depend upon the conduct of each one of us at this critical moment.

The "Special Order of the Day," issued by Field-Marshal Sir Douglas Haig on April 11, 1918

The United States had no large army to send immediately. It would take months to recruit and train young men to fight in Europe. Meanwhile, the situation in Europe looked desperate for the Allies. In the autumn of 1917 the Italian army collapsed at Caporetto and, after two retreats, only managed to hold a line because of massive support from British and French troops. In November 1917, as you read on page 11, the British offensive at Passchendaele collapsed completely. In the same month the Bolsheviks gained power in Russia. Their leader, Lenin, made it clear that he would take Russia out of the war. In March 1918 the Treaty of Brest-Litovsk ended all fighting on the Eastern Front. This meant that thousands of German soldiers were free to fight on the Western Front. The German High Command realized their best chance of winning the war had come. They had to defeat the Allies before fresh, well-trained, and well-equipped American troops arrived in Europe.

On March 21, 1918 the German attack began with a massive assault on the British and French lines between Arras and La Fere.

Within half an hour German troops had broken through the British front lines. They pushed the British troops back over the old Somme battlefield. Within a week the Germans had advanced 36 miles into France. By early April 1918 the German front line was only 48 miles from Paris and the city again lay under threat. However, the German soldiers were exhausted. Too many men had gone too far, too quickly. Now the Allies hit back.

SOURCE 18

Over there, over there,
Send the word, send the word over there,
That the Yanks are coming, the Yanks are coming,
The drums rum-tumming everywhere.
So prepare, say a prayer,
Send the word, send the word to beware.
We'll be over, we're coming over,
And we won't come back till it's over, over there.

An American song written by G. M. Cohen in 1917

SOURCE 17

What impression did this poster sent to Britain by the United States in early 1917 try to give the British people?

PERSHING'S CRUSADERS
AUSPICES OF THE
UNITED STATES GOVERNMENT
·THE FIRST OFFICIAL AMERICAN WAR PICTURE·
TAKEN BY U.S. SIGNAL CORPS AND NAVY PHOTOGRAPHERS

THINK IT THROUGH

World War I didn't only take place on the Western Front. Why, then, was this the only front to which America sent troops?

A small number of American soldiers arrived in Europe in July 1917, but it took a long time before there were enough troops to make any impact on the Western Front. In May 1917 the USA introduced **conscription**. Within a month over ten million men had registered for the army. From March 1918, about 250,000 American soldiers arrived in Europe each month. By the end of the war more than four million men were in the American army, nearly half of them in Europe. The United States had more fighting men in Europe than Britain did.

At first the Americans fought as a separate army under General Pershing. Then things changed. The Allies realized that the German army was making a tremendous push on the Western Front, and that they had somehow to force them back. Together with Pershing, the Allied commanders Pétain and Haig came to an agreement. Instead of fighting as separate armies, backing each other up when necessary, they would fight under one supreme command. General Foch would be the supreme commander of the Allied troops in Europe. For the first time, battle plans would be coordinated. This worked well at the Second Battle of the Marne in July 1918. French, Moroccan, and American troops, using hundreds of tanks, pushed the Germans back over the Marne. Though no one knew it at the time, this was the beginning of the end of the war.

On August 8, 1918, British, Australian, and Canadian troops broke through the German line and advanced 5 miles. On September 12, American troops destroyed the German salient of St. Mihiel, southeast of Verdun. The final battle began on September 26, when the Allies captured the Hindenburg Line (the strongest German trenches) and took 400,000 prisoners. As the Allies pushed the Germans further and further back, the German army was close to surrender. The German government, faced with the collapse of its army on the Western Front, the collapse of its allies in the East, and starvation at home, asked for peace.

SOURCE *19*

An American 14-inch gun being fired in the Argonne region of France in September 1918

SOURCE *20*

It was not so much what the American army did in 1918, but its potential if the war dragged on, that helped tip the balance in favor of the Allies ... the vast American potential, in material perhaps as much as in manpower, made it apparent to the German High Command that to press on with the war was simply suicidal.

*J. M. Winter, **The Experience of World War I**, 1988*

Wounded American soldiers being treated in an old church, Neuvilly, France, on September 26, 1918

Armistice

The USA did more than provide loans, food, raw materials, and soldiers to support the Allies. In January 1918 the President of the United States, Woodrow Wilson, announced the Fourteen Points, which he believed should be the basis for peace. The first five points suggested a complete change in the way governments dealt with each other. The other nine showed clearly that Wilson believed the war had happened because nations had ignored the right of every person to live in his or her own national home. These points were very **idealistic**, and some of them would not work out in practice. However, they did provide a basis for peace.

On October 3, the German Chancellor, Prince Max of Baden, asked President Wilson for an armistice, to be followed by a peace based on the Fourteen Points. Wilson consulted the Allied leaders. They did not see why Germany, who they thought had caused the war, should have an equal share in the new world promised by Wilson's Fourteen Points. Meanwhile, the situation in Germany worsened. Bulgaria, Turkey, and Austria signed armistices with the Allies; the navy mutinied at Kiel; influenza swept through the country, killing thousands of people who were already weak and starving. Riots flared up and the Communist Red Flag flew over many buildings. On November 9 the Kaiser fled to Holland. Two days later, in a railway carriage in the forest of Compiègne in northern France, the armistice was signed. Germany agreed to the Allies' terms, which were far harsher than Wilson's Fourteen Points. The war was over.

WILSON

Thomas Woodrow Wilson (1856–1924) was elected Governor of New Jersey in 1910. He was elected President of the United States in 1912 and again in 1916. An election slogan was "He Kept Us Out of War." But Wilson was forced into war. In 1917 the United States declared war on Germany. In 1918 Wilson issued his Fourteen Points, which he hoped would be the basis for peace. He went to the Versailles peace conference in 1919, but the US Senate refused to ratify [agree to] the peace treaties. The United States withdrew from European politics.

What Was Trench Warfare Like?

SOURCE 1

The York and Lancaster Regiment in a front-line trench, January 12, 1918. Two men are checking and cleaning a Lewis gun on the firestep. One soldier is pouring himself a drink of water from a jerrican. One man is alert, watching the enemy through a box periscope.

The trenches

In France and Flanders the "front line" was not a line but a complex system of trenches. The typical front-line trench was a fire trench. Trenches were deep enough to keep out shrapnel, but snipers could always kill the unwary soldier. The floor was covered with wooden duckboards, and a firestep enabled soldiers to fire at ground level. There was usually a forward sap, or listening post, out into No-Man's-Land. A second line of trenches was built in the same way as a support line, linked to the front-line trenches by communication trenches, which ran back to reserve trenches.

Some front-line trenches were well built and defended; others were less so. The French usually built deep dugouts under the support trenches, and rarely had reserve trenches. The Germans built far deeper, stronger trenches than the Allies. They had reserve and support trenches, and usually had a line of machine-gun emplacements, protected by concrete, behind the front line.

SOURCE 2

If you want to find the old battalion,
I know where they are,
I know where they are.
If you want to find a battalion,
I know where they are,
They're hanging on the old barbed wire.
I've seen 'em, I've seen 'em
Hanging on the old barbed wire,
I've seen 'em,
Hanging on the old barbed wire.

A song sung by soldiers during World War I

The land between enemy trench systems was a terrible place. It was called No-Man's-Land. Sometimes No-Man's-Land was 880 yards wide; sometimes only 77 yards. It was pitted with shell holes and littered with abandoned equipment, unexploded shells, and rotting bodies, which stretcher parties could not find. Unless there was a battle going on, No-Man's-Land was a quiet place during the day. At night, things changed. Wiring parties repaired the tangled rolls of barbed wire which protected the fire trenches and tried to improve defenses; patrols crawled out in the mud and filth to **reconnoiter**; sometimes raiding parties crept across to the enemy lines to kill or capture prisoners for interrogation. During a battle, stretcher parties crawled out to rescue the wounded and dying and to bring back the dead.

SOURCE 3

Whether they did this on purpose to show how lucky we were and had nothing to fear, whether they did it to cheer us up, or whether they really thought they were correct, I don't know. But they made a huge mistake; a wicked mistake. There's no doubt about that.

> *Russell Bradshaw, Eleventh East Lancashire Regiment (the Accrington Pals), complains about the standard instructions to cross No-Man's-Land at a walking pace.*

SOURCE 4

The need to cross No-Man's-Land at a good pace, to reach the parapet before the enemy could reach it, was not discussed. Each man carried nearly half his body weight, which made it difficult to get out of a trench, impossible to move much quicker than a slow walk or to rise and lay down quickly.

> *B. H. Liddell Hart, **History of the First World War**, 1972*

SOURCE 5

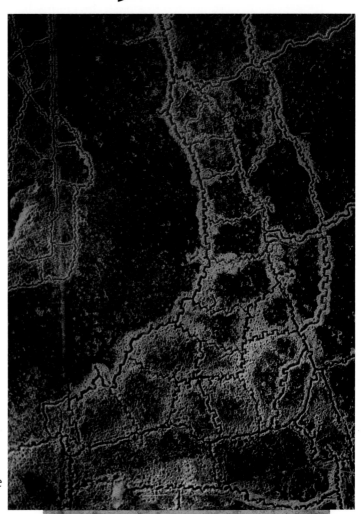

An aerial photograph of the Western Front between Loos and Halluch, at 7:15 P.M. on July 22, 1917. The British lines are to the left; the German lines are to the right. No-Man's-Land is the black strip curving between the two trench systems. The trenches leading off the picture top right and center are the German communication trenches. The whole area is pockmarked with shell craters.

COPPARD

George Coppard (1898–   ) joined the army in 1914. In France he kept a diary, against army rules. In 1968 he used it to write *With a Machine Gun to Cambria*.

Artillery and Infantry

Heavier guns were needed to smash the enemy barbed wire entanglements, destroy enemy guns, and prepare a way through for the attacking troops. Each German corps, for example, had at least twelve 150mm heavy howitzers. Trench mortars were developed, which fired almost straight up into the air. The number of heavy guns grew and grew. In 1914 the French had 300; by 1918 they had about 7,000, of which approximately 300 were mounted on railway carriages so they could be moved easily. By 1918, Germany had around 8,000 heavy guns. The largest of them, nicknamed "Big Bertha," shelled Paris from a distance of 90 miles. (Look back, too, to Source 19 on page 14.)

Each side made heavy bombardments before a battle. The aim was to destroy the enemy's barbed wire and front-line defenses. But heavy bombardments warned the enemy to expect an attack. The element of surprise was lost. By 1917 "hurricane" bombardments were used. These were quick, violent, and took the enemy by surprise. Bombardments also destroyed roads, farms, churches, marketplaces, houses, and schools. Often, when the infantry finally managed to break through enemy lines, they simply didn't know where to go.

About 21 million men were wounded during the war. The enormous number of casualties were caused in part by the destructive powers of new weapons, including the machine guns.

SOURCE 6

The real test was the barrage. Some hid their heads in their greatcoats. Some wept; others joked hysterically. But all shook and crawled, white faced in dull endurance. "How long? How long?" men would ask themselves again and again. Men had no choice but to last out, nerves pared to the bone.

From Denis Winter, Death's Men, 1978

A barrage. At first guns were trained on enemy front lines. The gun barrels were gradually lifted higher and higher so that shells would land on support and then on reserve trenches. Later a "creeping" barrage was developed. This moved forward on a timed basis ahead of the soldiers.

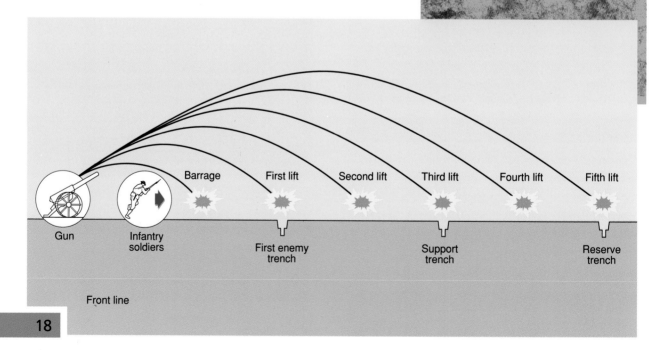

Gun — Infantry soldiers — Barrage — First lift — First enemy trench — Second lift — Third lift — Support trench — Fourth lift — Fifth lift — Reserve trench — Front line

Part of the city of Ypres in 1917. It was lost and regained by the Allies in 1914, and after that was bombarded until the end of the war. This is an official Australian photograph.

British soldiers used the standard Number Five Mills bomb, although some improvised by filling metal jam tins with explosive. Most infantrymen carried bayonets, which could be fixed to their rifles. However, judging by the casualty figures, not many seem to have used them. Much more effective were the fighting knives and home-made clubs used in trench raids.

Many infantrymen believed that the two most important weapons on the Western Front were shovels and machine guns. Shovels meant they could repair and strengthen their trenches; machine guns meant that they could defend their trenches against attacks. The problem was, of course, that both sides did the same.

Although all troops carried small-bore, high-velocity bolt-action, repeating rifles, these were not nearly as effective as machine guns. Riflemen could fire only 15 shots a minute, while one machine gun had the firepower of 60 rifles. At first, machine guns were clumsy and heavy, but they were quickly made lighter and easier to handle. The British had the Lewis gun, which weighed 29 pounds; the Germans the Maxim gun, which weighed 20 pounds. By the end of the war, Italians and Germans were using a very early type of submachine gun. In 1915 the British army set up a separate Machine Gun Corps, which by 1918 numbered 120,000 men.

It was sometimes possible to take out machine-gun posts by using grenades. The Germans used hand-thrown grenades, and grenades which were fired from rifles. Most

Communications

One of the greatest problems for infantrymen in battle was communication. Leading waves of attacking soldiers as they went "over the top," young officers were killed first. The smoke and noise and confusion of the battlefield separated men from their commanders. Senior commanders were usually miles behind the front lines, out of touch with what was actually happening. Orders were often lost or proved impossible to carry out because the situation changed so rapidly. Many generals simply refused to believe that battles weren't going the way they had planned.

SOURCE 8

Whatever the nature of infantry weapons used on the Western Front, the men who carried them were trapped in a war of futility and monumental suffering, the sources of which lie not in guns but in the minds of the men who sent them there.

J. M. Winter, The Experience of World War I, 1988

Gas and tanks

Obviously, the opponents needed new ideas to break through the stalemate on the Western Front. One of these ideas was to use poison gas. There was nothing really new in this idea, which had been suggested but never used in the Crimean War (1853–6) and the Civil War (1861–5). What was different about the use of poison gas on the Western Front was that the chemical industries of Britain, France, and Germany were now able to produce gas in large quantities in convenient containers.

The French were the first to use toxic weapons on the Western Front in August 1914, when they fired tear-gas grenades at German troops. Two months later the Germans bombarded the British with shrapnel shells containing a chemical irritant, disanisidine chlorsulphonate. In January 1915, German troops fired shells containing xylyl bromide at the Russians. Clearly both sides were trying to develop the "ideal" poison gas. Success came to the Germans in April 1915, when troops opened more than 500 cylinders of chlorine gas. The gas was carried on the wind to French soldiers, 5,000 of whom were killed and 10,000 injured. The British caught up quickly. In September 1915, at the Battle of Loos, they released chlorine gas against German troops. From then on, both sides used poison gas. In December 1915, phosgene, a choking gas, was first used by the Germans, who soon added to it diphenyl chlorasine, which made soldiers sick. Mustard gas, used by the Germans in July 1917, quickly became the most commonly used poison gas on the Western Front. It was colorless and didn't smell; it caused terrible vomiting and ate away at soldiers' lungs. All soldiers hated and feared all kinds of poison gas.

SOURCE 9

British machine gunners at the Battle of the Somme, 1916. They are wearing gas masks to protect against poison gas.

SOURCE 10

When I objected because the use of chlorine gas was a mode of warfare which violated [broke] the Hague Convention, he said the French had already started it by using rifle ammunition filled with gas. Besides, it was a way of saving countless lives, if it meant that war could be brought to an end sooner. After a training course I returned to Flanders as a front-line observer. Gas warnings were given a number of times, but the attacks had to be postponed again and again because of weather conditions. Every time the attack was fixed, the wind changed and blew toward us. The units brought up from the rear had to be taken back again. In the middle of April, High Command decided to remove the gas cylinders and take them to a sector of the front northeast of Ypres, where wind conditions were more favorable.

In January 1915 Otto Hahn was sent for by Geheimrat Haber from the German Ministry of War. Here Otto Hahn describes what happened.

The tank represented another attempt to break through the stalemate of trench warfare. A British army journalist, Lieutenant Colonel Ernest Swinton, designed a vehicle that could cross difficult ground. After trials with a variety of tractors, the first tanks finally appeared in 1916. They had caterpillar tracks and guns mounted at their sides. They were slow, difficult to steer, and sunk into soft ground, but they crushed barbed wire and could not be damaged by rifle fire.

In July 1916, the British used tanks for the first time at the Battle of the Somme. The 50 tanks either failed to start or got stuck in the mud. It was a different story in November 1917. At the Battle of Cambrai, over 400 of the new Mark IV tanks were used by the British. After three days they had driven a salient 5 miles beyond the Hindenburg Line.

The German High Command believed that to use tanks was a sign of weakness. It meant admitting that all proper military tactics had failed. Nevertheless, German field commanders were happy to use captured British and French tanks when they could. German tanks did not come into service until March 1918, when it was almost too late.

SOURCE 11

A British tank abandoned at Passchendaele in 1917

SOURCE 12

It was not so much the difficulty or the physical impossibility of breaking through trench lines that led to the war being such a protracted [long drawn-out] and bloody affair, but rather the fact that even a badly defeated army could rely on reserves, moving in by railway. The conscription of whole generations meant that manpower was, to all intents and purposes, inexhaustible.

N. Stone, an historian, wrote this in 1985.

VON LUDENDORFF

Erich von Ludendorff (1865–1937) joined the German army in 1882. By 1914 he had become a Major-General. On the Western Front he helped plan the German advance through Belgium and their capture of Liege. He was appointed deputy to Commander-in-Chief Hindenburg on the Eastern Front. They planned the destruction of the Russians at the battle of Tannenberg and the Masurian Lakes in August 1914. In 1916 von Ludendorff and Hindenburg were sent to work on the Western Front.

Von Ludendorff supported the ideas of Germany fighting defensively until 1917, using submarines unrestrictedly, and the terms of the Brest–Litovsky treaty with Russia. However, in September 1918, von Ludendorff advised opening peace negotiations. He resigned on October 27, and fled to Sweden in disguise.

In 1923 he was involved in Hitler's Munich putsch. He supported the Nazis, but became a pacifist at the end of his life.

21

What Was Life Like in the Trenches?

Digging a front-line trench was not easy. It took 450 men, guarded by marksmen, six hours to dig about 275 yards. Then the new trench had to be connected to the trench system by communications trenches. Duckboards, dugout frames, wooden boards, and thousands of nails held the soil back and made it possible to fight and live in the trenches. Soldiers did not stay in the front-line trenches for long, unless a battle raged. Then everyone had to stay and fight. Usually, however, only 2,000 of the 15,000 men in a division stayed at the front at any one time. In a typical month, a soldier would spend four days in the front-line trenches, four days in support trenches, eight days in the reserve trenches, and the rest of the time behind the lines.

New units arrived at the trenches at dusk. The soldiers being relieved would quickly explain where to find the dugouts, stores, telephones, and latrines. The officers would inspect the logbook and discover the state of the barbed wire, work in progress, and enemy shell and sniper activity. However, if the previous unit had lost a lot of men, parts of the trench system might well be destroyed, and such things as stores and telephones missing.

Some parts of the front line were very quiet. A soldier called Alec Waugh spent a month north of Bapaume in 1917; there no one was injured, let alone killed. Around Ypres, on the other hand, the fighting raged constantly. However, wherever the trenches were on the front line, a soldier's daily routine remained more or less the same.

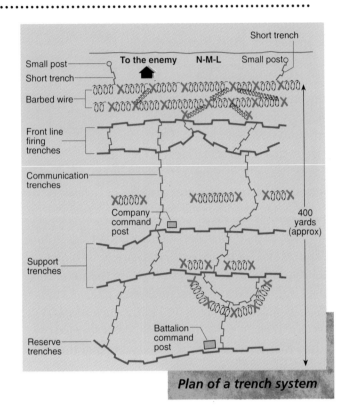

Plan of a trench system

What were soldiers doing when they were not fighting?

A soldier's day started about half an hour before dawn. The **night patrols** and **raiding parties** were back in the trenches by then. Roll was called and the orderly officer checked guns and ammunition boxes, the trenches, and stores. Everyone then ate breakfast, except the sentries, who ate later. After breakfast came the officers' inspection. Then the platoon sergeant gave out the duties for the day. About one-third of the men were put on sentry duty, one-third were sent back up the communication trenches for supplies, and one-third worked in the trenches, repairing and improving them if they could. The day ended at dusk, when the ration parties made their way back down the communication trenches with food, stores, packages, and letters from home.

Night in the trenches was a time of silence and fear. It was also a time of enormous activity. Men stationed in the **listening posts** out in No-Man's-Land gave early warning of enemy activity. Then they passed it back to their front-line trenches, so that the soldiers would be prepared. Listeners heard the enemy's coughs and sneezes, a sentry's shuffle, and footsteps on duckboards. The enemy seemed very near and sometimes they were. At any moment a German patrol might stumble upon the listening post, or a sniper pick off one of the listeners.

Night patrols crawled through No-Man's-Land, trying to pick up information about the enemy. Patrollers worked in pairs. They blackened their faces with burnt cork and equipped themselves with knives and clubs.

Raiding parties were different. Men and officers blackened their faces and took off all evidence of rank. Blackjacks were collected, knives and bayonets were sharpened, pistols and grenades readied. Then the raiding party set off for the enemy trenches. Their aim was surprise. They took prisoners if they could, and killed if they could not.

The real nighttime killers were the snipers, who worked in "nests" behind the front line, or in camouflage suits in No-Man's-Land. They worked in pairs: one was an observer, using a telescope and working out ranges; the other was a crack shot. Together they were a deadly team.

SOURCE 1

These soldiers are coming out of a communication trench near Arras. Cold, rain, and mud were formidable enemies too.

SOURCE 2

One night the quiet was broken by heavy shell fire. About five miles away, near Langemark, a raid or something of the sort was taking place. Artillery from both sides was firing hard. We could see the flames of the shells as they fell and hear the crump of the explosions. Gradually the panic spread. The whole salient woke up. More rockets, nearer now. Machine gun crews on both sides fired across No-Man's-Land, just in case. Wires were now busy to various HQs, inquiries were made, men were hustled from dugouts to trenches. The mania reached our front. Behind us a battery fired salvo after salvo. The German batteries replied. A raid had been carried out by troops to the right of Langemark. One prisoner had been taken. In half an hour all was quiet again.

M. Evans describes a nighttime incident when he was fighting on the Ypres salient.

What did soldiers eat when they were in the trenches?

On page 22 you read how every day, unless a battle raged, some soldiers were sent back up the communication trenches to collect rations. Soldiers put dry food, like sugar and tea, at the bottom of an empty sandbag. On top they put tins of jam and butter, stew, bully beef (a kind of corned beef), margarine, cheese, bread, and hardtack. Then, if there was room, came letters and packages from home. Each sandbag had a label tied to it, saying to which section of the front line it was to be taken. Sometimes the soldiers strapped screw-topped containers of stew and oatmeal to their backs. Everything needed at the front line had to be carried up the communication trenches, and usually at night. Food did not always arrive in good condition. Sometimes the ration parties came under attack from the enemy; sometimes they stumbled into shell-holes full of filthy water and rotting bodies. Sometimes it poured with rain and the sandbags got soaking wet.

For breakfast a front-line soldier might have hardtack, or hot oatmeal if he was lucky, some bread, margarine, and jam; for lunch, bully beef or stew and hardtack; for dinner, bread and jam. Usually there was plenty of hot, sweet tea made with condensed milk. Drinking water came in cans that sometimes had held gas or oil. All front-line soldiers had a drink of rum every morning at roll call. An extra ration of rum was issued just before an attack, to help the men make the first terrifying leap out of the trenches into No-Man's-Land.

The Eternal Question.
"When the 'ell is it goin' to be strawberry?"

*A picture from a magazine, **The Illustrated London News***

SOURCE 3

We ate our breakfast lying on our backs
Because the shells were screeching overhead.
I bet a rasher to a loaf of bread
That Hull United would beat Halifax
When Jimmy Stainthrope played full-back instead
Of Billy Bradford. Ginger raised his head
And cursed, and took the bet, and dropped back dead.
We ate our breakfast lying on our backs
Because the shells were screeching overhead.

A poem by Wilfred Gibson, who fought in World War I and survived

THINK IT THROUGH

Source 3 is a poem about eating breakfast in the trenches. Source 4 is a painting which is intended to make people laugh. Does either of these sources have a serious point to make? How can you be sure?

A working party of British soldiers on the Somme in November 1916

How did soldiers keep clean and healthy?

Soldiers found it extremely difficult to keep clean when they were in the trenches. Water for washing had to be brought up in two-gallon containers through the communication trenches. There was only one container for every 40 men. The last few would have to wash in filthy sludge. Sometimes soldiers heated up water so they could shave, but mostly they simply stopped shaving. Mud was everywhere. In dry weather there was dust. Mud and dust penetrated **puttees** and boots, raincoats, and overcoats. No one could change clothes in the front-line trenches.

Every trench had a latrine dug at intervals. Most men, however, preferred to use a pail or helmet and toss the contents into No-Man's-Land when they had finished. For toilet paper they used newspaper, grass, or the tail of the shirt they were wearing. British troops were amazed to discover that American troops, when they arrived, carried soft toilet paper rolls.

Because the men were dirty they became infested with body lice. Lice lived in warm places on a soldier's body. One soldier counted 103 lice crawling around his body and in the seams of his undershirt and underpants. Lice lived by sucking blood. Each louse laid five eggs a day, which looked like tiny grains of rice. The best way to kill a louse was by squashing it between thumb and forefinger. Another way was to run a lighted candle up and down the seams of clothes. The trick was to coagulate the blood of the louse without burning a hole in the shirt. Rats swarmed everywhere. They fed on leftover food and rotting bodies. Men in the reserve trenches at Mesnil reckoned they killed about 30 rats each night. Flies, too, were a problem. Each infantry division had about 6,000 horses. They produced about 40 tons of manure every day, which provided an ideal breeding ground for flies. One soldier counted 32 dead flies in his shaving water and 72 crawling between his shoulder and wrist.

Lice, rats, and flies spread disease. There was little that the soldiers could do to stop it. They scratched louse bites with dirty fingers, they ate food on which rats had urinated, they coughed and sneezed over each other, and they drank infected water.

SOURCE **6**

Anthrax	8
Dysentery	6,025
Enteric fever	1,275
Frostbite	21,487
Meningitis	692
Nephritis	15,214
Pneumonia	2,157
Tuberculosis	1,660
Venereal diseases	48,508

Hospital admission list for 1917, showing casualties that were not the result of enemy action

THINK IT THROUGH

By 1914 doctors knew about the connection between dirt, germs, and disease. Why, then, didn't they do anything about improving conditions on the Western Front?

25

The war was supposed to be over by Christmas 1914. The authorities had not, therefore, done very much about making arrangements for men to go home on leave. Troops were only occasionally given leave to return home for a break; officers went home more often. Where men spent their leave therefore became very important. Some went to a training camp at Etaples. Most found lodging with a French family, or took over houses, church halls, and barns. For the British and Americans, language was a problem. Very few soldiers spoke any French at all because they had not learned it at school. Some enterprising businessmen produced dictionaries and phrase books especially for the troops; one Belgian shipping company published a guide to *The Language of Three Allies*. Many soldiers (look at Source 7) took a less serious approach.

OUR RAPID FRENCH SYSTEM FIRST LESSON DEVELOP THE "SHOULDER-RAISE". IT WILL SAVE YOU LEARNING HUNDREDS OF WORDS, SUCH AS:— "YOU SURPRISE ME!" "I AM NOT SURPRISED" "I DON'T KNOW" "PERHAPS" "IT DOES NOT MATTER" "I DON'T UNDERSTAND" ETC. ETC. ETC

A drawing suggesting how British soldiers could overcome their poor knowledge of the French language

What did soldiers do in their time off?

The officers organized activities and entertainment for their men, and sometimes they joined in themselves. The authorities approved of these ways of spending spare time. Most soldiers played soccer. Behind the lines they organized soccer leagues and arranged tournaments. Towards the end of the war there were baseball leagues, too, for the Americans. Visiting actors put on plays, and sometimes the soldiers wrote and acted in plays themselves. This involved men dressing up as women, which invited rude comments from the audience. Various battalions put on concerts, and most organized sports days. The soldiers also had fun in ways the authorities did not like. Soldiers gambled, got drunk, went out with girls, and did everything they were used to doing as young men at home.

We entered the estaminet [a French café]. Soldiers were standing round the walls waiting for vacant seats. An oil lamp was hanging from the ceiling. In the middle there was a long table and soldiers were seated around it, squeezed tightly around it, eating eggs and chips and drinking wine and coffee. The air was hot and moist and smelt of tobacco, burning fat, and steaming clothes. There was a glowing stove at one end of the room. A woman with flaming cheeks was throwing handfuls of sliced potatoes into it while she held the saucepan in which the eggs were spluttering. The conversation was boisterous and vulgar, much of it at the expense of the woman, who laughed frequently and pretended to be shocked and called the soldiers "naughty boysss."

A soldier remembers his time behind the lines on leave

Almost every unit in the British army had its own magazine or newspaper. These were written by the soldiers. The most famous was the *Wipers Times*. ("Wipers" was British army slang for Ypres). It was first produced in February 1916 by men of the Sherwood Foresters, working in a dilapidated office near the Menin Gate.

The paper was often very rude, and poked fun at officers and the way in which the war was being run. It was rude about journalists who reported on the war without really understanding life on the front.

It also criticized civilians for their attitudes to the war, and tried to make the politicians look silly.

All soldiers sang songs. They sang when they were marching, and they sang when they were working; they sang when they were having a beer, and they sang at concerts. Some of their songs were very rude, some were very funny, and some (look back at Source 2 on page 16) might seem sick. Many could be sung to hymn tunes or to the tunes of popular songs.

SOURCE 9

I WORE A TUNIC

I wore a tunic, a dirty khaki tunic,
And you wore your civvy clothes,
We fought and bled at Loos; while you were
  on the booze,
The booze that no one here knows.
You were out with the wenches while we
  were in the trenches,
Facing an angry foe,
Oh, you were a-slacking, while we were
  attacking
The Germans on the Menin Road.

AND WHEN THEY ASK US

And when they ask us, how dangerous it was,
Oh we'll never tell them, no, we'll never tell
  them:
We spent our pay in some café,
And fought wild women night and day,
'Twas the cushiest job we ever had.

And when they ask us, and they're certainly
  going to ask us,
The reason why we didn't win the Croix de
  Guerre,
Oh, we'll never tell them, oh, we'll never tell
  them
There was a front, but dammed if we knew
  where.

THE BELLS OF HELL

The bells of hell go ting-a-ling-a-ling
For you but not for me,
The little devils how they sing-a-ling-a-ling
For you but not for me.
Oh death, where is thy sting-a-ling-a-ling
Oh grave, thy victory?
The bells of hell go ting-a-ling-a-ling
For you but not for me.

FORWARD JOE SOAP'S ARMY

Forward Joe Soap's army, marching without
  fear
With our old commander, safely in the rear.
He boasts and skites from morn till night,
And thinks he's very brave,
But the men who really did the job are dead
  and in their grave.
Forward Joe Soap's army, marching without
  fear,
With our old commander, safely in the rear.

Songs from World War I

THINK IT THROUGH

These songs have a serious as well as a fun message. (Look back to Source 2 on page 16.) What is the serious message?

27

Keeping in touch

British soldiers had little chance of getting home on leave. This made contact with friends and family back at home in "**Blighty**" even more important. All soldiers needed to know that they had not been forgotten by those they cared about; they needed to know, too, that somewhere beyond the mud and the horror, normal life continued. However, not all the correspondence was, or could be, truthful. The people at home were urged not to tell husbands, brothers, cousins, and friends any bad or depressing news; letters from the front to friends and relatives back home were **censored** by the authorities.

SOURCE 10

I am now using a new pony
Nothing seems to do any good
To my old pony, which still
Remains lame in spite of
All bandages. The pony that
I have belonged to our origi-
Nal padre, who has left us
For the Base camp at Havre.
On completing this year he
Returns to his parish. He had
Merely six weeks until then,
And the authorities decided to
Retain him in France. It didn't
Seem worthwhile to Employ him with us,
And then
Immediately send him back.
Last night we had a
Long rumor that a gen-
Eral had been assassinated.
Sorry that I have no news!
　　　　　Yours aye
　　　　　　Jock

A letter from Second Lieutenant J. Macloed of the Queen's Own Cameron Highlanders. Can you crack the code?

SOURCE 11

NOTHING is to be written on this side except the date and signature of the sender. Sentences not required may be erased. If anything else is added the post card will be destroyed.

[Postage must be prepaid on any letter or post card addressed to the sender of this card.]

I am quite well.

I have been admitted into hospital
{ sick } and am going on well.
{ wounded } and hope to be discharged soon.

I am being sent down to the base.

I have received your { letter dated _____
{ telegram „ _____
{ parcel „ _____

Letter follows at first opportunity.

I have received no letter from you
{ lately
{ for a long time.

Signature }
only }

Date_____
Wt.W65—P.P.948. 8000m. 5-18. C. & Co., Grange Mills, S.W.

A British field postcard: soldiers at the front were allowed to send only these cards home. Many soldiers tried to say more by crossing out letters to make new words.

SOURCE 12

I am not allowed to tell you where I am, because the General is afraid you might tell someone at school, and he might tell the German master [teacher], and the German master might telegraph the Kaiser and tell him. And then, of course, the Kaiser would send an airplane to drop bombs on us.

Part of a letter from Color-Quartermaster-Sergeant Robert Scott Macfie to his young nephew.

TEAR OUT THIS PAGE AND KEEP IT FOR REFERENCE.

PACKING TOMMY'S CHRISTMAS PARCEL.

THE Christmas puddings and cakes must be made early this year if Tommy is to come in for *his* share. Parcels intended either for *Egypt* or *Salonika* must be posted so as to reach London not later than 12*th* November, whilst parcels for France must be posted early in December.

If you wish to send the parcel by *post*, it must not weigh more than 7 lbs. The postal rates to France are a shilling for parcels weighing not more than 3 lbs., and for parcels weighing more than 7 lbs. 1s. 4d. The first rate also applies to parcels intended for Egypt, but for the parcels weighing between 3 and 7 lbs. the rate is 1s. 9d.

FOR VERY BIG PARCELS.

NO doubt, however, you will want to send a bigger parcel at Christmas, and in this case—if the parcel is to be sent to France—you should send it "C/o the Military Forwarding Officer, Southampton Docks." If it is intended for Malta, it must be sent "C/o the Military Forwarding Officer, Avonmouth," and must reach there not later than November 20th. Parcels intended for Gibraltar should also be sent to Avonmouth, but they can be sent up to December 1st.

It is most important, however, that you should make sure that your parcel does not weigh less than 11 lbs., as otherwise the package, however it is addressed, will be treated as a gift for the troops generally. The maximum weight allowed is 56 lbs.

Suppose, however, you happen to have two or more friends in the same unit, you may send a *small* parcel—or parcels—under cover of a large parcel (that is, one weighing between 11 and 56 lbs.), provided the covering parcel is addressed to the Officer Commanding the unit. He will see that the various parcels are distributed to the men concerned.

HOW TO PACK THEM.

BROWN paper and ordinary cardboard must *not* be used in packing the parcels. Even if the boxes are of soft wood, the box must be bound with hoop-iron unless the contents are very light. It is necessary, therefore, that your gifts should be packed in strong boxes, sacking or other strong material.

Stout labels, clearly addressed, are another necessity. So much so indeed that the War Office now undertake to supply suitable labels, which can be had on application to the Secretary, War Office, Whitehall, London, S.W. 1. This label is made of very strong Manilla and measures 6 in. by 3 in. The address, name of sender, contents of parcel, and the words, "C/o Military Forwarding Officer, Southampton," should, however, also be painted on the package itself. These special directions only apply to parcels over 11 lb. in weight, not going by Parcel Post.

The carriage on these parcels should be paid to Southampton Docks, from which no further carriage will be charged.

WHAT TO PUT INSIDE.

NOW something about the actual contents of the parcel. You must remember that there are certain military regulations to be borne in mind with regard to the sending of certain goods to the various fronts.

For instance, safety matches may be sent, but only if they are packed in sealed tins or tin-lined cases. Cakes, puddings, and jams should also be packed in tins. No fresh fruit, vegetables, or other goods of a perishable nature may be sent, the only exception to this rule being in the case of apples, onions, carrots, and turnips, and even these must be specially selected and carefully packed. These exceptions only apply to parcels sent to France.

As to the things you *may* send, a good deal, of course, depends upon Tommy's individual requirements, and you will know your own Tommy's special needs better than I. There are some things, however, that are universal favourites "out there," and the Y.M.C.A. have told me some of the things that Tommy has confided to them that he specially looks for in his parcel from Blighty.

One of these reveals the fact that Tommy really *does* like jam—provided it is *not* plum and apple! A pot of black-currant or strawberry jam is always acceptable. Apples, condensed milk, cocoa, and chewing-gum, are also favourites.

So much for eatables. As to other things, you will generally find that he likes a candle or two, some soap, patent pipe-lighter, pencils, and packets of stationery, and, of course, socks and mufflers.

*From a magazine, **Women's Weekly**, published in 1917.*

I'm thinking, Mrs. Atkins, now that Tommy's gone away,
You'll be sending a letter from Home.
Don't tell him all your troubles, though for instance yesterday
The children's boots you bought took half your separation pay.
The eldest boy wants trousers and the rent is overdue,
You're planning and you're scheming for of debts you've got a few!
But don't you write and tell him, for here's my advice to you
When you send him a letter from Home.
Send him a cheerful letter
Say that it's all OK.
Tell him you've ne'er felt better
Though it's all the other way.
Don't send a word of sorrow,
Send him a page of joy,
And don't let your teardrops
Fall upon the kisses
When you write to your Soldier Boy.

Popular song on the Home Front, 1916.

THINK IT THROUGH

It seems as if when soldiers on the Western Front wrote home, they couldn't tell the truth. It seems as if when friends and relatives wrote to soldiers on the Western Front, they were encouraged to lie if things were bad. Why, then, did people bother to write to each other at all?

Did Allied and German soldiers hate each other?

The official Allied army attitude to the Germans was clear. All Allied soldiers had to fight to win, and this meant killing German soldiers. Army intelligence units wrote propaganda posters that encouraged soldiers to hate the Germans so killing them would be easier. These posters contained stories of various atrocities. The stories might once have had a grain of truth in them, but they had usually been hugely exaggerated. Some soldiers, however, did not need any encouragement to hate. They might, for example, be in a regiment that was well known for its fierceness in battle and with a tradition of toughness. They might come from a family with a tradition of soldiering and to whom hating and killing an enemy in battle posed no problem. Some soldiers might have more private reasons to hate the enemy: perhaps a dearly loved brother or friend had recently been killed. Indeed, soldiers' diaries and memoirs show clearly that mostly the enemy was disliked, sometimes hated, and almost always feared. However, some soldiers found time to reflect on what they were doing to other human beings.

SOURCE 16

A Scots Guardsman giving a wounded German prisoner a drink after an attack, August 1918

SOURCE 15

A German section were lying fully exposed to us on level ground where they had remained from the moment daylight caught them and they were shunning death like the masses around them, but small movements and their regular formation gave them away. We put bullets into the heads of the lying enemy. Two or three of them rose stiffly to their knees to escape but the bullets caught them and they flopped down again. I felt disgusted. We had slaughtered too many already. I was miserable until the German line was still and I prayed for them as I killed them.

A British soldier remembers an incident on the Western Front.

SOURCE 17

The ordinary soldier knew quite well in his heart that at bottom Fritz [English nickname for a German] was much such another as himself.

Canon E. C. Crosse, who was a British senior chaplain on the Western Front

Many soldiers, however, found that they could respect and admire their enemies even though they disliked and feared them, too. There were agreed, and totally unofficial, cease-fires along the Western Front on Christmas, 1914. German and Allied soldiers met in No-Man's-Land for games of soccer and to trade souvenirs (Source 18). At many points in the war the fighting stopped, too, to let both sides bury their dead. There was a general, and again unofficial, agreement that neither side would shoot at the other during roll call at dawn. Sometimes enemies would shout messages to each other, make jokes, and even send over necessities like hardtack. Indeed, there were parts of the front line where an unofficial truce held for months at a time. The authorities, of course, disapproved.

SOURCE *18*

We had a very cold but quite cheerful Christmas Day in the trenches and even a slice of plum pudding. And though you might not believe it, we had a truce for a day just along our bit of the line. Somehow or other we arranged with the Germans opposite to stop fighting until midnight on Christmas night; all Christmas Day we were walking about outside in front of our trenches. The Germans came out of theirs and we met halfway and talked and exchanged souvenirs, our own bullets for theirs. They also gave some of our fellows cigars of which they said they had plenty and we gave them tins of bully beef as they said they had very little food. A great many of them spoke English and one said he had been a waiter in London. On Christmas Eve they were singing away as hard as they could go and they had lights all along their trench in front of us.

Part of a letter home written in January 1915 by Warwick Squire, a private in the London Regiment

SOURCE *19*

After we had been in the trench for about an hour, four Germans came over and gave themselves up. They were shaking all over with cold or fright. I tapped my revolver and said: "Sie verstehen?" [Do you understand?] and they said: "Jawohl!" [Certainly]. I started telling them that I had been a student in Germany, and so enjoyed talking German again that I quite forgot that we were in trenches and very close to the Boche [a word of contempt for the Germans used by French and British]! War is so very strange and stupid when the people doing the fighting do not hate each other at all. War is the stupidest thing in the whole world.

Written by Second Lieutenant E. F. Chapman, Twentieth Royal Fusiliers, in November 1916, during the last phase of the Battle of the Somme

JOFFRE

Joseph Jacques Cesaire Joffre (1852–1931) joined the French army when he was eighteen years old. He fought in North Africa and Indochina and, in 1914, was made commander of the French armies in France. He organized the winter attack at the battle of the Marne. Soldiers and politicians both trusted him. He wanted to wear the Germans down rather than fight big battles, but was forced into the battles of Verdun and the Somme. Both of these battles were especially disastrous for the French. Joffre was removed from active command on December 31, 1916, and replaced by Robert Nivelle. However, he was still used as an adviser.

How Did Soldiers Cope with Casualties and Death?

SOURCE 1

All the armies fighting on the Western Front were large; casualty figures were enormous. This posed huge problems for military medical services. Not only did they have to move thousands of wounded men away from the battlefields as soon as possible, but they also had to provide hospitals where the soldiers could be treated. In addition, they had to recruit and train the medical officers, doctors, and nurses needed to cope.

A badly wounded man being carried through the trenches. He died 30 minutes after this photograph was taken.

What happened to wounded soldiers?

At night, after a battle, stretcher parties searched No-Man's-Land for wounded men. No-Man's-Land, as you read in the previous unit, was a terrible place. The stretcher parties usually worked in the dark, stumbling over dead and rotting bodies, sometimes falling into slime-filled shell holes, as they tried to reach wounded men. Sometimes the wounded men were unconcious or too weak to call out for help. Finding them could be a matter of luck. Many soldiers were horribly hurt when they became entangled in massive barbed wire defenses in front of the German lines. It was often impossible to save them. Sometimes stretcher parties tried to get to wounded men during daylight hours. Then they worked under covering fire from their own side. Some men who were not too badly hurt managed to make it back to their own front line.

All wounded men needed help quickly. They were taken back through the communication trenches to first-aid posts, where regimental medical officers gave what help they could. They sorted out which soldiers simply needed a dressing on a split head or cut leg and could be sent back to the front line, and which soldiers needed further treatment. Those who needed further treatment were sent to casualty clearing stations. These were mobile hospitals a few miles behind the lines. Only the really heavy artillery could reach them, and so they were reasonably safe. In the early days of the war, soldiers were taken there in horse-drawn ambulance wagons. Later, ambulances with gasoline engines were used. Soldiers who were too sick to be moved further and those who needed an immediate operation stayed at the casualty clearing station. The rest were sent to

Captured German doctors dress the wounds of British soldiers.

base hospitals, far behind the lines. There they were nursed until they were well enough to fight again. Some British soldiers with really severe wounds were sent home to 'Blighty' and were cared for in British hospitals and nursing homes.

What kinds of wounds did doctors and surgeons have to treat?

High-velocity bullets and shrapnel produce severe wounds. They tear into flesh and shatter bones. In order to protect their heads, Allied soldiers began wearing steel helmets. These became standard issue in 1916. Even so, ten percent of all injuries were to soldiers' heads. Surgeons developed expertise in operating on soldiers' eyes, faces, ears, noses, throats, and brains. Many of them became highly skilled in bone surgery.

Many wounded soldiers had lain in the filth and mud of the battlefield before being picked up by a stretcher party. The fields of northern France were well manured and fertile. Bacteria entered soldiers' open wounds, and many wounds became infected with gas-gangrene and tetanus. Infections like these challenged the surgeons because they had to be cleared up before surgery could be effective.

Scientists and technicians worked hard to help doctors and surgeons. After a couple of years most casualty clearing stations were supplied with X-ray machines for finding bullets and shrapnel. Blood transfusions, too, began to be used. Often these involved direct transfusion from the donor to the wounded soldier. As the war progressed, techniques for storing blood were developed.

THINK IT THROUGH

Doctors and surgeons learned a lot from their work during the war. Does this mean that in some ways the war was a good thing?

What happened to soldiers who had been gassed?

Once the troops began using poison gas, the workload for doctors and nurses increased tremendously. The medical services of all armies together dealt with about 1.5 million gassed soldiers. About 9,000 soldiers died from the effects of gas poisoning. Gassing caused blindness, deafness, loss of voice, difficulty in swallowing, difficulty in breathing, burns, and a high fever. Some of these conditions were temporary; others remained with soldiers forever. Some gases had a delayed action. They affected soldiers' lungs and air passages about an hour after they had been inhaled. The soldiers then often developed pneumonia. This meant that one or both of their lungs filled with fluid. Unless pneumonia was treated immediately, and this was difficult on the Western Front, their lungs were damaged forever.

Both the painting on the front cover and the photograph (Source 3) show men suffering after a gas attack. Which do you think makes the bigger impact, the photograph or the painting? Why?

Men suffering the effects of a gas attack, taken by Tom Aitken, a British official photographer, at the advanced dressing station in Bethune, April 1918

SOURCE 3

What was shell shock?

Most men at the front suffered from strain, stress, and exhaustion. Nothing in their lives before they got to the trenches had prepared them for what happened there. This was true for conscripts and volunteers, who had perhaps worked in stores or on farms before they enlisted. It was also true for experienced soldiers. Nothing like it had happened before. Some soldiers simply could not cope with the horrors they saw every day. Their eyes twitched and their hands shook. Some could not hear or speak; others moaned, screamed, or shook violently whenever they heard gunfire. Some men cracked suddenly; for others it was a slow process because they got support from friends or from doing a particularly responsible job. Whenever it happened, this sort of mental collapse was called "shell shock."

By August 1915, many officers and soldiers admitted to a hospital were sent back home suffering from shell shock. The army called in psychiatrists to help. By the end of 1916 there were four special centers for shell shock victims in northern France. They were set in quiet countryside and staffed by kindly medical officers. Most men recovered and went back to the front. Some were sent back home for further treatment. Some never recovered. Later, many men received army pensions for the effects of shell shock. Thousands of men, though not mentally ill enough for an invalid's pension, suffered from nightmares and other terrors for the rest of their lives.

Illnesses

On the Western Front men caught typhoid and dysentery from drinking infected water. Body lice carried typhus fever, and they helped the spread of a new disease, trench fever, which was very like influenza. Another new condition was "trench foot," which was developed by thousands of soldiers. Their feet swelled up to twice their normal size and went completely numb. Only when the swelling began to go down did the soldiers begin to feel almost unbearable pain.

SOURCE 4

His steel hat was at the back of his head and his mouth slobbered, and two comrades could not hold him still. These badly shell shocked boys clawed their mouths ceaselessly. Others sat in the field hospitals in a state of coma, dazed as though deaf, and actually dumb.

A soldier describes shell shock. From Eye Deep in Hell by J. Ellis, 1976

SOURCE 5

This British cartoon was called The Secret Invader. During World War I, soldiers were killed by diseases as well as by the enemy.

Death

All soldiers lived with the sight, sound, and smell of the dead and dying. Some of the dead and dying were friends and companions; some were strangers; some were enemies. Thousands were killed in battles by shelling and thousands more mown down by machine guns. Hundreds of soldiers were killed by trench-raiding parties and snipers. The fear of death and of the death of friends were amongst the worst things a soldier had to put up with.

SOURCE 6

Just then the Germans started shelling. I told the CO I had left my horse on the track, and he let me get away at once. I found Sammy and he made a beeline for the road. Shells were bursting right along the track, but Sammy did not once falter. He took those huge holes in his stride and I thanked God he could jump. After what seemed like an eternity, we reached the road. Sammy swerved down it but fifty yards on he skidded to a halt in front of a convoy of motor vehicles. I stood up and waited for Sammy to rise. He didn't move. I looked at him closely. One of the side bars of the saddle had been shot away and there was a nasty wound in Sammy's rump, also several other wounds in other parts of his body. I could see no sign, however, of a fatal wound anywhere, but he was undoubtedly dead. The lorry driver helped me pull his body to the ditch on the side of the road. I was in tears. Sammy had brought me safely through that terrific barrage without a scratch, but at the cost of his own life. And I had to leave him there in a ditch. I shall never forget him.

Soldiers did not just weep for the death of friends. Bombardier Alex Dunbar of the British Royal Field Artillery remembers the death of his horse, Sammy.

SOURCE 7

The dead man lay amidst earth and broken timber. Never before had I seen a man who had just been killed. A glance was enough. His face and body were terribly gashed as though some terrible force had pressed him down, and blood flowed from a dozen fearful wounds. The smell of blood mixed with the fumes of the shell filled me with nausea. Only a great effort saved my limbs from giving way beneath me. I could see from the sick, gray faces of the men that these feelings were generally shared. A voice seemed to whisper with unchallengeable logic: "Why shouldn't you be next?"

A soldier remembers seeing his first dead body. From Death's Men by Denis Winter, 1979

SOURCE 8

A British chaplain saying a prayer for a dying German soldier. This photograph was taken at an advanced dressing station during the Allied advance of September 1918.

Courts Martial

Some soldiers were shot by their own side. This happened accidently, when creeping barrage arrangements went wrong or when a sniper mistook for the enemy a soldier crawling across No-Man's-Land. Shooting was also done deliberately. Many soldiers ran away. They deserted for many reasons. Some were afraid, some had shell shock, and some had problems at home they needed to solve. Most deserters had quite simply had enough. When deserters were found they faced a **court martial**. In the British army a major, captain, and lieutenant judged the prisoner. The prisoner's own **adjutant** prosecuted him and a company officer defended him. During the war 304,262 British soldiers were court martialed this way. A total of 346 were shot as a punishment. A firing party of twelve men would be chosen at random from the soldier's own battalion. The men were issued with mixed live and dummy bullets so no one would know who had fired the fatal shot. The prisoner would be taken away to a quiet place, usually at dawn, and shot. Not all soldiers shot at dawn were deserters. Some had committed crimes like murder and rape.

SOURCE 9

A man was shot for cowardice. The volley failed to kill. The officer in charge lost his nerve, turned to the assistant provost-marshal and said, "Do your own bloody work, I cannot." We heard later that he was arrested. Officially this butchery has to be applauded but I have changed my ideas. There are no two ways. A man either can or cannot stand up to his environment. With some, the limit for breaking is reached sooner. The human frame can only stand so much. Surely, when a man becomes afflicted, it is a case for the medicals. How easy for the generals living in luxury well back in their chateaux to enforce the death penalty and with the stroke of a pen sign some poor wretch's death warrant. Maybe of some poor, half-witted farm yokel, who once came forward of his own free will without being fetched. It makes one sick.

A soldier writes of his feelings about a court martial death sentence he watched being carried out during World War I. From Death's Men by Denis Winter, 1978

HAIG

Field Marshall Sir Douglas Haig (1861–1928) trained at Sandhurst to be a British army officer. He served as a cavalry officer in the Sudan (1885) and South Africa (1899–1902). He then served in India and by 1914 he was a general. He led the First Army Corps of the British Expeditionary Force in France. He fought at Mons, on the Meuse, and at Ypres.

In December 1915 he replaced Sir John French as Commander-in-Chief, Western Front. But Haig was a cavalry officer. He did not understand how to fight a war with infantrymen. His one tactic was to attack over and over again, no matter how little was gained or how many died.

He had the support of King George V, but clashed with the Prime Minister, David Lloyd George, who accused him of wasting soldiers' lives. Lloyd George trusted the French general, Robert Nivelle, more than he trusted Haig. But, despite a severe defeat in 1918, Haig kept calm. He agreed with the appointment of Marshall Foch as commander of all the allied forces and worked with him for victory in 1918.

After the war, Haig was made an earl. He spent the rest of his life organizing help for injured soldiers, and for the widows of those who had been killed in the war.

What Part Did Women Play on the Western Front?

Women did not fight on the Western Front with machine guns and artillery, nor did they dig trenches or stagger up the communication trenches with sandbags full of soggy rations. Even if the women had wanted to, the authorities would never have permitted such a thing. At first the government did not allow any women, apart from nurses, to work near the front. As the war went on, more and more men were needed to fight. The government reluctantly allowed women to do other sorts of work, such as drive ambulances. Between 1914 and 1918, over 25,000 women worked behind the front lines in Europe, Africa, and Asia. Most of the women worked on the Western Front with some kind of official organization.

SOURCE 1

A VAD nurse dresses the hand of a wounded German prisoner in the VAD dressing station at Abbeville in June 1917. Dressing stations gave immediate help to the wounded. More serious cases were sent down the line. This was the nearest a VAD worker would come to the front line.

FANYs

In 1907 the First Aid Nursing Yeomanry (FANY) was founded by a group of rich upper-class young British women. They were interested in the romantic and rather impractical suggestion made by a Sergeant-Major Baker that groups of nurses should be prepared to ride out to battle fields to give first aid. They wanted adventure, they owned their own horses, and they trained hard. During World War I, FANYs joined forces with the Red Cross. They left nursing to other groups, and concentrated on ambulance driving and motor maintenance. They gained a reputation for the high quality of their work. By 1918 there were 116 FANYs working behind the front lines in France.

VADs

The Voluntary Aid Detachment (VAD) was begun in 1909 with the aim of training voluntary nurses who would be available if Germany invaded Britain. The VADs were unpaid, so they came from middle- and upper-class families. Early in 1914 a list was drawn up of VADs who were willing to work overseas if there was an "emergency." During the war, over 8,000 young British women went to northern France. They worked as nurses, orderlies, and drivers. In 1916 the military authorities began paying VADs $80–$120 a year. In return, VADs agreed to cook and do clerical work and storekeeping, as well as nursing. The help and support given by VADs to the regular army medical staff was enormous.

At least a third of the men were dying: their daily dressings were not a mere matter of changing huge wads of stained gauze and cotton wool, but of stopping bleeding and replacing intestines and draining and re-inserting numerous rubber tubes. I often wonder how we were able to drink tea and eat cake in the operating theater, in the fetid stench, with the thermometer about 96 degrees [Fahrenheit] in the shade, and the saturated dressings and yet more gruesome human remnants heaped on the floor.

*From **Testament of Youth** by Vera Brittain, 1933. She was the daughter of a wealthy Staffordshire manufacturer. She was studying for a degree at Oxford University when she decided to become a VAD nurse. Her fiancé, Roland Leighton, and her brother Edward were killed in the war.*

WAACs

Many soldiers were working for the army in France as cooks, orderlies, bakers, and mechanics, and were not actually ready to fight. To release men from those sorts of jobs, and to enable them to fight, the War Office and the Government agreed that women should be employed by the army.

The Women's Army Auxiliary Corps or WAAC (later called Queen Mary's Army Auxiliary Corps) was organized like the army. Controllers and administrators (officers) were paid between $480 and $2000 a year; all other women were paid according to the work they did. This meant that, unlike women in FANYs and VADs, the women who applied to the WAAC came from all social classes.

By the end of March 1917 more women had applied than were needed. The first group of WAACs started work in France on March 31, 1917. Although the women did release soldiers to fight, it is difficult to be certain exactly how many men were freed in this way.

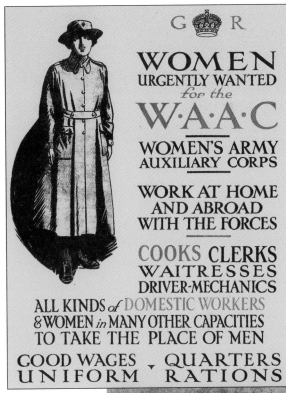

A British government poster asking women to volunteer for the WAACs

The army reckoned that four women WAACs were the equivalent of three soldiers. WAACs worked in army canteens and bakeries; they worked as telephone operators and clerks; they worked as storekeepers and cooks; they ran army printing presses. By November 1918 over 40,000 women had joined the WAACs. Not all of them worked behind the front lines in France. Some worked in Britain, but always with the idea that the work they did for the army meant that a soldier could go and fight.

THINK IT THROUGH

Why would women want to go and work on the Western Front where it was dangerous?

The "Women of Pervyse"

In August 1914 Mairi Chisholm, from an aristocratic Scots family, went to London on her motorbike. There she joined the new Women's Emergency Corps and worked with them as a dispatch rider. She was noticed by Sir Hector Munro, who was planning to take doctors, drivers, and ambulances to Belgium. A great feminist, Munro wanted to take four women as well, to prove that they were as good as men on the battlefield. The four women he chose were Helen Gleason, an American whose husband was working in Flanders as a freelance journalist; Dorothy Fielding, one of the daughters of the Earl of Denbigh; Elsie Knocker, a widow and nurse who later married a Belgian aristocrat; and Mairi Chisholm.

Mairi Chisolm and Elsie Knocker look after a wounded soldier, at Ramscapelle, September 11, 1917

For two months Chisholm worked with Hector Munro's team behind the front line in Belgium, as an ambulance driver. Then Elsie Knocker asked Chisholm to work with her on a separate project. Knocker had realized that soldiers were dying from shock while they were being taken by ambulance to hospital. Her idea was that she and Chisholm would set up a first-aid post immediately behind the front line. Chisholm agreed. Immediately the two women began working in Pervyse, which was virtually on the front line. Knocker and Chisholm worked under fire and in appallingly dangerous conditions. They rescued wounded men from No-Man's-Land; they went out to the trenches to bring the wounded back to Pervyse; they treated soldiers who were brought in to their first-aid post. They also provided the men with soup and hot drinks before sending them back up the line to base hospitals. Apart from visits home, they stayed in Pervyse from November 1914 until they were gassed early in 1918.

Knocker and Chisholm were known as the "Women of Pervyse." They were each awarded the British Military Medal for "gallantry and devotion to duty in action," and the Belgian Order of Leopold.

What a wonderful and terrible day. I shall never forget it. We started at Berlaese and were there during the bombardment. Then on to Appels for some wounded. Left the car by the roadside and walked four miles over meadows to the trenches by the river. Germans other side of river. We saved a Major and a soldier—the latter with foot blown off and back shot—both very bad. Had to sneak back in the dark under fire—a terrible journey in the rain with two men so bad. Found Tom with the car had also been under fire—Germans fired Berlaese village, a great glow in the sky—a long weary ride back, very tired and cold. Both wounded arrived safely but soldier died later.

From Elsie Knocker's diary, October 5, 1914

SOURCE 6

We worked a lot for the Royal Naval Air Service and the Royal Flying Corps. They used to be brought down in No-Man's-Land and we used to have to make expeditions to try and get the pilots out. That's where we got the Military Medal, you see. It was really for our work in getting hold of these pilots who came down in front of the trenches. We went on foot, not always with stretchers, just hoping to be able to get them with their arms around our necks.

From an interview with Mairi Chisholm, 1976

SOURCE 7

A recruiting poster published during World War I by the Essex County Recruiting Committee. This is just one of the ways in which Edith Cavell's death was used by the British.

Edith Cavell

In 1914 Edith Cavell was forty-nine years old. She was the director of the School of Nursing in Brussels, the capital city of Belgium. When Belgium was invaded by the German army, Brussels was put under German military law. Cavell continued nursing. She believed it was her duty to care for sick and injured people, whether they were enemy or allied soldiers. Nevertheless, she did help over 200 Allied soldiers to escape from Belgium. They had been trapped behind German lines after the British retreat from Mons. The Germans found out what she had done. Cavell was arrested for sheltering the soldiers and tried by a German military court. She was found guilty and shot. The British authorities used her death in anti-German propaganda. They presented her as a brave heroine who was an innocent victim of German cruelty.

PANKHURST

Emmeline Pankhurst (1857–1928) was born Emmeline Goulden, In Manchester, England. In 1879 she married an attorney, Richard Marsden Pankhurst. He wrote the first Women's Suffrage Bill and the Married Women's Property Acts of 1870 and 1882. In 1889 Emmeline founded the Women's Franchise League and in 1902 (with her daughter, Christabel) the Women's Social and Political Union. Their members campaigned hard for votes for women. She emigrated to Canada in 1918.

During the war, Emmeline Pankhurst encouraged women to join the armed services or to work in industry. Women who worked on the Western Front (and back in Britain doing jobs that had previously been done by men) did a great job to help to persuade men that women should be given the vote.

How Is the Western Front Remembered? Poems, Plays and Paintings

Poetry

World War I inspired many poems. Most of these poems were written by soldiers who fought in the trenches. Many of the young poets were killed before the end of the war. Some of the survivors also wrote poems afterwards. All of the poems tell us something about life and death on the Western Front and elsewhere. Some of the poems on these two pages, and elsewhere in this book (see page 24), are parts of poems; others are complete. They tell us what poets felt about the war. They tell us, too, what the poets wanted us to believe.

Returning, We Hear the Larks

Somber the night is.
And though we have our lives, we know
What sinister threat lurks there.

Dragging these anguished limbs, we only know
This poison-blasted track opens on our camp—
On a little safe sleep.
But hark! joy—joy—strange joy.
Lo! heights of might raging with unseen larks.
Music showering on upturned faces.

Death could drop from the dark
As easily as song—
But song only dropped.

By Isaac Rosenberg (1890–1918). He fought in the trenches and was killed.

For the Fallen

They went with songs to the battle, they were young,
Straight of limb, true of eye, steady and aglow.
They were staunch to the end against odds uncounted:
They fell with their faces to the foe.

They shall not grow old as we that are left grow old:
Age shall not weary them nor the years condemn.
At the going down of the sun and in the morning
We will remember them.

By Laurence Binyon (1869–1943). He was in charge of the Oriental paintings department at the British Museum during World War I.

A Dead Statesman

I could not dig; I dared not rob;
Therefore I lied to please the mob.
Now all my lies are proved untrue
And I must face the men I slew.
What tale shall serve me here among
Mine angry and defrauded young?

By Rudyard Kipling (1865–1936). His son was killed in the war.

Futility

Move him into the sun—
Gently its touch awoke him once,
At home, whispering of fields unsown.
Always it woke him, even in France.
Until this morning and this snow.
If anything might rouse him now
The kind old sun will know.

Think how it wakes the seeds,—
Woke, once, the clays of a cold star.
Are limbs, so dear achieved, are sides,
Full-nerved,—still warm—too hard to stir?
Was it for this the clay grew tall?
O what made fatuous sunbeams toil
To break earth's sleep at all?

By Wilfred Owen (1893–1918). He fought in the trenches and was awarded the Military Cross. He was killed one week before the war ended.

Battlefield

Yielding clod lulls iron off to sleep
bloods clot the patches where they oozed
rusts crumble
fleshes slime
sucking lusts around decay.
Murder on murder
blinks
in childish eyes.

January 1915

By August Stramm, translated from the original German.

Aftermath

Do you remember the dark months you
    held the sector at Mametz—
The nights you watched and wired and
    dug and piled sandbags on parapets?
Do you remember the rats; and the stench
Of corpses rotting in front of the front-line
    trench—
And dawn coming, dirty-white, and chill
    with hopeless rain?
Do you ever stop and ask, "Is it all going to
    happen again?"

Do you remember that hour of din before
    the attack—
And the anger, the blind compassion that
    seized and shook you then
As you peered at the doomed and
    haggard faces of your men?
Do you remember the stretcher cases
    lurching back
With dying eyes and lolling heads—those
    ashen gray
Masks of the lads who once were keen
    and kind?
Have you forgotten yet?...
Look up, and swear by the green of the
    spring that you'll never forget.

Written by Siegfried Sassoon in March 1929

THINK IT THROUGH

Wilfred Owen was killed in 1918. Many unfinished jottings and poems were found among his papers. This is something he wrote:

> **"All the poet can do today is warn. That is why the true poets must be truthful."**

Do you agree that this is what this war poetry does? Or does it do something more or different?

Plays and films

Oh! What a Lovely War is a play about the First World War. It tells the story of the war through the songs and documents of the time, and aims to show some of the stupidity, pointlessness, and horror of trench warfare. The play was first performed by Joan Littlewood's Theater Workshop in London in 1963. Six years later a film version was made by Richard Attenborough. Both the play and the film were great successes.

This is a still from the film **Oh! What a Lovely War**. It shows Sir Douglas Haig (played by John Mills). His "successes" are shown in the endless field of crosses behind him.

SOURCE 2

They were only playing
   leapfrog,
They were only playing
   leapfrog,
They were only playing
   leapfrog,
When one staff officer
   jumped right over
   another staff officer's
   back.
One staff officer jumped
   right over another staff
   officer's back,
And another staff officer
   jumped right over that
   other staff officer's back,

A third staff officer jumped
   right over two other staff
   officers' backs,
And a fourth staff officer
   jumped right over all the
   other staff officers' backs.
They were only playing
   leapfrog,
They were only playing
   leapfrog,
They were only playing
   leapfrog,
When one staff officer
   jumped right over
   another staff officer's
   back.

This is a song from World War I, and was sung in the film **Oh! What a Lovely War**, while Sir Douglas Haig (acted by John Mills) played leapfrog with his staff officers.

ROSENBERG

Isaac Rosenberg (1890–1918) was the son of Jewish people who emigrated from Russia to Britain. They lived first in Bristol, then in London. In 1904, Isaac became an engraver's apprentice. In 1911 his mother paid for him to go to the Slade School of Art. In 1912 he published his first book of poetry. In 1913, despite his family's pacifist views, he joined the army. He was killed in the trenches.

Paintings

This painting is called **We Are Making a New World**. It was painted by the British war artist Paul Nash.

This painting is called **Merry-Go-Round**. It was painted by the British artist Mark Gertler after the Battle of the Somme in 1916.

OWEN

Wilfred Owen (1893–1918) left Britain to teach English in Bordeaux, in France, but came back to enlist in 1915. He served as an officer in the Artists' Rifles and the Manchester regiment. He fought in France, but caught trench fever and was sent to Edinburgh, Scotland, to recover. In 1918 he returned to France, where he fought bravely and won the Military Cross. Owen was killed on the Sambre Canal just one week before the Armistice was signed.

Time Line: The Western Front

1914

Aug. 9–17	BEF lands at Boulogne, France
Aug. 24	Battle of Mons
Aug. 26	Battle of Le Cateau
Sept. 5–10	First Battle of the Marne
Oct. 12–Nov. 11	First Battle of Ypres

1915

Mar. 10–13	Battle of Neuve Chapelle
Apr. 22 –May 24	Second Battle of Ypres
May 9	Battle of Aubers Ridge
May 12–15	Battle of Festubert
Sept. 15–Oct. 16	Battle of Loos
Dec. 17	Sir John French replaced as Commander-in-Chief of the BEF by Sir Douglas Haig

1916

Feb.–Dec.	Battle of Verdun
July 1–Nov. 18	Battle of the Somme

1917

Apr. 6	United States declares war on Germany
Apr. 9–16	Battle of Arras
July 31–Nov. 10	Third Battle of Ypres
June 17	Battle of Messines Ridge
July	First American troops arrive in Europe
July 15–Nov. 12	Battle of Passchendaele (part of Third Battle of Ypres)
Fall	Collapse of the Italian army at Caporetto
Nov.–Dec.	Battle of Cambrai

1918

Jan.	President Wilson announces his Fourteen Points as a basis for peace
Mar.	Treaty of Brest-Litovsk ends Russian involvement on the Eastern Front
Mar. 21–July 15	German offensive on the Western Front
Aug. 8–Sept. 29	Allied offensive
Sept. 29	Hindenburg Line captured by the Allies
Nov. 9	German Kaiser flees to Holland
Nov. 11	Armistice signed

Glossary

adjutant an army officer who works with a senior officer

Allies countries who join together to fight a common enemy

Blighty soldiers' slang for home (usually England or Britain)

British Expeditionary Force the name given to the first British troops to go to France in 1914

Cabinet a group of ministers in charge of deciding what the government should do

censor remove parts from a book, letter, or photograph, to protect a country's security

conscription compulsory military service, forcing men to fight for their country

court martial a special army court

diversionary attacks attacks that are intended to draw away the enemy

flamethrowers machines that used either gas or paraffin to make a flame that burned the land ahead

idealistic based on ideas of perfection instead of on ideas about what might be possible

listening post the end of a small trench in No-Man's-Land, where one or two soldiers would sit very still, listening for enemy activity

mobilize get ready to fight

munitions weapons and ammunition

night patrols groups of soldiers who blackened their faces and crept out into No-Man's-Land at night to find out what the enemy was doing

offensive beginning of a campaign or battle

outflank go around the side of something, usually enemy troops

puttees long strips of cloth wound around a soldier's legs for protection

raiding parties groups of soldiers who crossed No-Man's-Land at night and raided the enemy trenches

reconnoiter to map out the land, usually before troops advance

salient a bulge in a line of attack or defense

stalemate a situation where neither side can make a move

Index